I0132735

# Letters
## to the
# BROKEN

## Living Is Still an OPTION

**Dareyelle Avant**

Published by

Emerge Publishing Group, LLC
Riviera Beach, FL
www.emergepublishers.com
561.601.0349

Dareyelle Avant 2018
Letters to the Broken

Printed in the United States of America

# *Contents*

# *Contents* (cont'd)

# *Acknowledgements*

I want to first thank my Lord & Savior before I thank anyone else. Without my Creator, none of this would be possible. I want to thank my parents, my loved ones, my friends, and kind strangers who have motivated and supported me throughout my 24 years of living. I truly believe "support gets supported" when it's genuine and coming from the heart. I love you all.

# DAREYELLE AVANT

*Letter*
*1*

# *Open Letter*

The purpose of this book is to let you, myself, and others know that healing is still available to us. No one makes it through this thing we call 'life' alone. Whether you are spiritual or not, healing and encouragement is what all of us need sometimes. Without hope we are nothing and without faith we have nothing to look forward to. Letters to the Broken/Living is Still an Option addresses issues many are uncomfortable discussing or afraid to address. The gap between love and hate is lack of understanding. You cannot heal what you do not speak. Just because you are broken doesn't mean you are not valuable or qualified to seek peace. It is during our broken times that we realize how much God loves us and discover who we are. Furthermore, when reading each letter, I simply ask that you read them with an open mind and a clear heart; even if you do not agree with a subject at least try to understand. Everyone whom I've addressed in this book is human, and therefore, as a Christian or just as a decent human being, we have an obligation to treat people with love, kindness, and respect. The truth of the matter is, it is very unwise to criticize a person's steps if you have never walked in his or her shoes.

I love you.

*Letter 2*

# *To the Broken Man*

Being a man consists of constant lessons which have to be learned. Sometimes I believe you allow society to create this idea of what a man should be instead of allowing God to mold you into the person you need to be. It bothers me to see how so many of you allow society to put pressure on you which has no business being there. You see, it is the lessons and the mistakes in life which mold you into the person you need to become. This letter is for the man who's trying to learn how to be a father, for the one who turns to the streets for validation, for the one who is angry, and for the black men who allow their brokenness to authenticate who they are.

In order to be a great man you have to first understand how you are molded. God created you with His bare hands; therefore, you are constructed. It is imperative for you to be mindful of what you allow to build you up and tear you down. You are not as emotional as women but you are not emotionless. Some of you really think it is illegal to cry and because of that thought, you are filled with anger and unstable emotions. Your anger does not get you anywhere. You can be angry because of your father or mother not being in your life, a woman breaking your heart, the dysfunction around your house or within your family, or simply because you are unhappy with where you are in life. No matter what the reason is, your destiny is not tied to your past hurts. Be the person you needed when you were younger. In other words, if you grew up without a father, be the best one you can be now. There are a lot of single dads around the world who do not get the credit they so rightfully deserve. You are appreciated and deserving of praise because only a real man can be a real father to his children.

Now, when it comes to the streets, it has nothing to offer you, brother. Instead of becoming a dope dealer, become a hope dealer. I understand the resources may not be available to you all the time, but you are the best version of yourself. Invest the money you make into something positive. Green is not the only way to survive; it is the cancer to why so many people are in debt not just financially but humanly as well. I am not judging you because surviving can become all we are, but living where hope seems fatal is also as powerful as surviving. I know the environment you live in is not always livable and it seems unorthodox to ask you to learn how to live around a hopeless place, when your family may be unhealthy and your house is not stable, but live anyhow. The best way to live is through the existence of your mind. Your mind has the ability to make you feel free even if your circumstance does not necessarily symbolize hope. It is in the mind where your freedom is made.

Furthermore, I understand as a man the last thing you give away is your heart. Every man is not a cheater and the ones who are the purest in heart seem to get their heart broken the most. Listen beloved, just keep loving and the right woman will come. Just because society has double standards, it doesn't mean you have to succumb to them. A real man only needs one rider since a good woman is the backbone to building your success. Be loyal to her just like you want your homeboys/friends to be loyal to you. Do not allow one heartbreak to keep you from loving the right woman for you. It is not worth losing what you have for a temporary arousal. You are meant and deserving of being happy. It is nice to come home when you have a rough or long day to a woman you know has your best interest in heart.

To my black men, I love you. You have every right to be angry sometimes but channel the anger in a positive manner. You are kings who are the anchor of the world. You are not thugs, gangbangers, dangerous, inconsiderate, and hopeless. You are kind, strong, thoughtful, creative, and Chief Executive Officers. Though your face may be touted as rappers, comedians, and athletes, you are also doctors, lawyers, activists, news reporters, movie directors, college graduates, great fathers, and so much more. You do not have to sell your soul to be recognized. Without you, some businesses and colleges wouldn't be successful or even exist for that matter. So, do not allow anyone to brainwash you as if your success is because of them, because it's not.

Be your own man and do not forget where you come from; if you do not return to help, then who will? Everyone is not always able to get out of tough circumstances like you did; sometimes a different pathway has to be created for them to flourish. As a black man you have the power to change how this world operates. The world does not fear the view they portray you as, but they fear what you can become and can accomplish if you ever grasp how powerful and valuable you really are; especially when you stick together as one.

Killing your own brother does not help the vision, but destroys the divine purpose. You are a king, so adjust your crown and sit on your throne. The only way things will get better is if you start making it better. God saw fit to create you first, so start acting like your reflection and not the tools people gave you so you can destroy yourself and your communities.

I love you all, no matter your race or color. I simply ask for you to be mindful of what you portray yourself as, since you are important to how the world is structured. When men become active in a positive way, change is birthed.

Sincerely,

Construction

*"It is our duty as men and women to proceed as though the limits of our abilities do not exist."*

Pierre Teilhard de Chardin

*Letter*

*3*

# *To the Broken Woman*

You are the production of all life. The first home of every human being was inside a woman. Now granted every race gets treated differently but the foundation of who you are as a woman is the same. A woman is what makes the world go around, but yet sometimes the emotions that cloud our thinking start to disrupt our peace. In other words, negative emotions have no right to interrupt your serenity. You are more than your body and your worth does not come with a price tag.

As a woman, there are many obstacles you may have to conquer. This letter is for the woman who has had an abortion, the ones filling a void with the wrong things, the single mothers, and for the woman who feels as though the world is on her shoulders, especially if she is a woman of color. With that being said, black women should understand we are the merchandise of strength. Everything we do matters. At times it seems as though the world allows us to be everything else but vulnerable. We are intelligent, beautiful, and strong and there is nothing wrong with us. However, we are human. It's okay to let go of the bitterness, the anger, and negative vibes that can build within us since it is not our identity.

To the woman who has had an abortion, many may judge you for your decisions; however, I will not. People see your decision but I see your brokenness. Any woman who thinks about giving up her child, has a broken spirit lingering inside of her. Therefore, I'm asking you to give yourself permission to forgive yourself. I don't know what your circumstances were at the time and even now in the present; but, understand the smallest things in life can bring forth a meaningful life. As women, the gift of love is already activated within us; we just have to embrace it.

To the ones who are filling a void with the wrong things, understand only peace and Heaven can fill that void Baby Girl. No matter what you do or say, your value becomes compromised when you allow someone else to validate who you are. God did not intend for people to complete us but wanted people to complement our completeness. Stop allowing your emotions to lead you to more probable heartbreaks. Starve your negative cycles and feed the energy you want to attract in your life.

Finally, to my single mothers, you are amazing! My only request is that you take some pressure off yourselves. You're only doing the best you can with the tools you have. Being a woman is not easy, but being a mother is the greatest job you will ever have. You are the co-partner of our Creator. He found your body worthy enough to be a mother. I know it may get hard sometimes, but, I ask that you stop working off of your own strength and start investing in God's strength. Remember, being broken doesn't make you weak; it reminds you of your humanity. You are appreciated.

I love you.


Sincerely,

Valuable

# *To the Broken Emotions*

It's amazing how much we allow our emotions to affect us. As a matter of fact, we can become intoxicated with them. Depression is one of the most common unhealthy feelings among people. Many of us, if not all of us, have experienced depression at some point in our lives; and if it is severe you may have to deal with it forever. However, you are not defined by depression or any negative feeling for that matter. You are defined by how you choose to view yourself and life despite the invisible weight (depression) you may have to carry. Get the help you need in order to fully enjoy your life.

Anger is another emotion which is capable of blocking our blessings. Suppressed anger is hurt. One cannot co-exist without the other; life will not allow it to. Many times people act out because of the unstableness of their emotions. One cannot be spiritually healthy and emotionally unbalanced; both have to be balanced. This is not implying perfection, but recommending steadiness.

As humans, I realize life will hit you off-guard more than it will confront you head on. In other words, one masters life when one understands the game of life. Life is like chess, every move matters; you have to do your best to protect your heart (which is the queen) and your mind (which is the king). I've come to the realization that our emotions become fragmented when we do not equip ourselves with the right tools. You cannot win a mental battle with emotions; the enemy will destroy you if you do. You have to speak things as though they were, in order to win. You also have to nurture your emotions; your soul depends on it. For example, depression can come from lack of healthy coping skills, the pride of not wanting to ask for help when you have experienced something traumatizing and the lack of understanding of what your soul needs. Some people conquer depression for good, and others learn how to stabilize it so that it does not dictate their life. No matter what emotion you are dealing with, remember the mind can be a terrible master, or a wonderful servant. Get your mind right, and a well-balanced life will follow.

I love you.


Sincerely,

Stabilizer

*Letter*
*5*

# To the Broken One (suicide)

I hear your pain. I see your pain. I am your pain. You want to give up, right? Throw in the towel? Well, let me just say I won't let you do that. I understand you're hurt; I recognize you have no hope, and I acknowledge you are exhausted but I won't let you throw in the towel. I love you too much to let you do that. Life is not easy, but my God is it worth it. You can find happiness with having less and joy from pain. In other words, if you can find anything to be happy for, or in, then use it as fuel to keep pushing forward into better days; even rain produces growth.

I have two questions for you. How can you stop living when you never started in the first place? How can you live when all you have been doing is surviving? Sometimes as humans we can endorse our feelings to bury us alive, and then become puzzled to understanding why we cannot breathe. It's difficult to breathe when we become crippled by our emotions and when we give our pain permission to erase our vision of what life can bring. Life can be fun, enjoyable, and bring fresh air to our bones. However, I do recognize it can also bring forth a lot of pain, sorrow and grief, but if you can feel then you can heal. Healing hurts sometimes. However,    the pain you are experiencing during this process is not trying to execute you; it is trying to free you.

Beloved, if you can knock down those walls that are trying to block you from reaching your peace, then there is hope for you to see the light at the end of the proverbial tunnel. It starts with your mind. Once you conquer your mind, you have conquered the world. It's the thoughts in our head which can manifest to our hearts and transfer to our actions that hinder us from living. If your thoughts are negative, your universe is negative. If you can make the decision to take life day by day while asking the Lord to hold your hand, then you can make it. As long as you have breath in your body, you have purpose living inside of you. However, when it is all said and done, if you do not want to live, then, find something you want to live for.

I love you.


Sincerely,

Healer

# *To the Broken World*

When reflecting on life what do you envision? When will you realize that money, fame, and selfishness do not get you far in life? You treat me like trash as if I never gave you the resources to be valuable. You put garbage on my back, drug me with pollution, and then express shock when I throw up what you put in my system. The days seem to be getting hotter and at times, you cannot tell the difference between the seasons; however, I hold back my full wrath to what you really deserve.

You are my reflection and I am in the hands of the Creator, so behave like your purpose. You are beautiful beyond measures. I give you oxygen to breathe and provide rain and sunshine for you to grow crops. I give you different views for you to enjoy and an ocean for you to profit from. You need me to survive and I need you to stay pure. When did money become the new earth? When will you all realize that money cannot stop tornados, earthquakes, and storms beyond your control? The earth you live on now was a gift given to you and as your Mother I am asking you to help me, for the day may come when I will no longer be your mother but just nature.

I love you.

Sincerely,

Mother Nature

*Letter*
*7*

# *To the Oppressor*

I want to keep this as respectful as possible because you too are broken. Anyone can be an oppressor. An oppressor takes advantage of someone simply because they can. When someone is able to dehumanize another human being, they gain this illusion of thinking they have a right to make someone else feel inferior. Being an oppressor is not just a black or white thing, it's a human blur within the mind of mankind. In this letter, I will discuss general oppression, my ancestors' oppression, and the reflections of oppressors.

Generally speaking, slavery still goes on today, not just physically but mentally as well. How can you treat someone as if their value didn't come with a price? How can you walk around every day as a Christian or a good person and never address the issues that occur within the world? Denial and silence is another form of oppression. We live in a time where we rather deny than acknowledge. We rather stay comfortable in the secrecy of our being than to transform into the spirit we as human beings were created to be. You look at someone's skin-tone and you judge them by their color but not by their character. I believe it will be wise for all of us to not underestimate the power of Denial, especially since it has the ability to change the narrative of someone's pain.

At this time, I would like to be transparent and admit that I cannot speak for other races; however, I can speak about my own. Being Black in America is not easy, nor is it comfortable all the time. There has always been a gap in understanding between blacks and whites. The method has always been, "to keep the body, but take the mind." The only thing black people want is equality and when we are denied the one thing we want, the conscious ones are seen as the bad guys. Truth can only crack the surface of healing; it does not hinder the purpose of growth. Blacks or any person of color is seen differently by those who are not white or a person of color. It is 2018 so why are people of color who live in Libya, Africa being beaten and traded to

Europeans who happen to be white; and no one seems to be doing anything about it except filming the tears of the broken and the unheard. There is a serious problem within the heart of man. It is the year 2018, and for America to elect a racist, insensitive, non-Christ-like, unkind person in the White House that my black ancestors built is a slap in the face. I understand many of us were not born into slavery but it doesn't mean we are not affected by its history. If you are not a person of color, your history affords you privilege, while my history could never afford it.

Look at our country and our world, people. Keep this in mind America, a young boy who was 12 years old was playing with a toy gun in a park. Although he was only a kid, he was murdered by police officers who never paid the price for what they did. This is not a pity party, this is the reality people of color have to deal with every day. When a person of color speaks out and they are an athlete, they risk losing their livelihood or endorsements. However, a person can retweet offensive things to many races but becomes president; not only does he become president, he remains president with no accountability towards his actions. The White House is in turmoil, no matter what party you represent; both political parties are the biggest gangs and biggest threat to mankind. Many would rather remain loyal to someone in their political party even if it cost them the dignity of their soul. The White House has no sympathy towards the people's tears that actually make this country run. The country can only reflect the leadership America put in charge.

It seems perfectly fine for a black athlete to run or dribble a ball, but when they speak about injustices that affect their communities, death threats and the depth of many people hearts start to be revealed. An athlete can put on and take off a jersey but they cannot take off their skin color or stay blind to the reality of systematic racism. Overall, no race should be systematically oppressed just because he or she is molded differently. We all bleed red and it should also be notified, not all white or non-white people are racist; there are more people blending together in the streets who care about the issues others are facing; it's just not publicized enough.

Finally, black people, stop forgetting what is inherited in your DNA. You have royal blood running through your veins. You are beautiful inside and out and you define who you are, not negative stereotypes. As a whole I ask that you stop oppressing each other. Stop degrading your own kind to be accepted by those who only tolerate you for your gift, not because they actually appreciate who you are. You are more than an athlete or a rapper; you are an entrepreneur, a doctor, a mother, a father, a lawyer, an educator, and so forth.

To the young ones who think the streets are the only parents you have to raise you, understand the only way out is through knowing what tools they gave you to destroy yourself. If you are a black millionaire or billionaire invest in the hoods that raised you or in communities who helped guide you to a better path. No one can make it on their own; and it frustrates me how so many people have this selfish mentality that it is not their responsibility to help others when they make it. If you are a Christian--as a Child of God---you have an obligation to help the less fortunate and if you are just a good person with no religious affiliation, it is your responsibility as a human being to at least give back to the source that helped develop you into the person you are today.

Overall, I hope and pray for everyone to do better. We do not have to live this way. There is a better way for us to handle things and approach uncomfortable issues. Love and acknowledgment with progressive actions is the key to a better world. We are one and I pray one day we all will start acting like it. I love you but oppression is wrong no matter who you are.

Sincerely,

Acknowledgement

*Letter 8*

# To the One Who Lost an Angel (children, loved ones, and best-friends)

Death always brings life. As paradoxical as this sounds, when one dies the opportunity of a more peaceful life is offered up. Losing someone is never easy. As human beings, we naturally grow attached to things and people, even though we know earth is our temporary home. When someone loses a child, a parent, a close friend or relative a part of them seems to die as well. In all honestly, I wish I can tell you, you will get past the loss or get over some deaths, but you won't. Some deaths you just learn to cope with and acquire a sense of peace as life goes on.

There is no amount of words or any scriptures at the time that will do your pain any justice. Only time and prayer can heal those wounds. Sometimes you have to travel to your peace in order for you to live in peace. You only get one mother and one father and when one loses a child the pain is unbearable. However, I want you to know you can still live and prosper from a broken place. Those broken places in your life are not meant to keep you down but to help develop you to a more beautiful strength only a few can get to.

So, I want to encourage you to keep going, not because you don't have a right to give up but because you have an obligation to live anyhow. True peace is not the absence of chaos but owning serenity in the midst of it. Better days are ahead.

I love you.

Sincerely,

Peace & Better Days

*"College can be a place where you find out who you are, and who you want to be."*

*SWAG*

*Letter*
*9*

# *To the Broken College Student*

Many say college is the best years of your life. However, what many might not tell you are the lessons you will learn that do not happen inside the classroom. I am not saying to take your teachers for granted and devalue the importance of a degree. What I am saying is to pay attention to the person you are while you are transitioning into a new version of yourself.

College will and can take a toll on you physically, mentally, spiritually, and emotionally. College is another world in and by itself; in the college world you figure out who you are, who you were, and who you would like to be. This is where dreams come true and manifest the potential of its purpose; this is also the place where you see the hustle of other people who make connections to add to their dreams.

Overall, college is the place where your pain will give you permission to be more understanding. Understand your faith can be tested, your endurance will be increased, your mind will become a battlefield, and your heart will go through constant surgery. It will be the heartbreaks that bend you the most and the hurt that will change your perspective on life. School will become overwhelming at times due to papers that have to be written and exams that have to be taken. Through it all, you have to remember why you are doing it. Pay attention to the lessons behind the trials which seems unbearable. A lesson will continue to present itself until you pass it. Be your own person and stop letting other people think they have the right to validate who you are. Do not be afraid to lose people along the way since college and life is not a race; it is a marathon. Know the heartbreaks will not kill you, the brokenness will not weaken you, your emotions can be conquered, and your mind can become a positive force to be reckoned with. College should be and can be an enjoyable experience but it also has the ability to change you; however, these lessons become more valuable when you allow it to change you for the better.

Sincerely,

Lessons

*"If it doesn't challenge you, it won't change you."*

*Fred Devito*

*Letter*
*10*

# To the Injured

Time adjusts all wounds. It's easy to take things for granted when you have access to it all the time. We do not only do it when it comes down to other people, but we also do it when it comes to our body. We do not like when things get misplaced or broken because it makes us have to relearn our body condition, one's patience goes under construction, and our mind and heart go into battle. You never know how strong you are until being strong is the only option you have left.

Sometimes life will injure your heart and leave your heart wounded; then the phrase, "My heart is broken" will linger in your head. Your heart is not literally broken but someone or some tragedy made you feel as though it did get shattered. Our heart is one of the most unselfish organs we have functioning through our body. It has the ability to keep loving even when people and life has disappointed it so many times. Some may view this as weakness but in all honesty, it takes real courage to love even when people give you valid reasons to stop being so loving.

Now to my athletes, I understand the sport you play is either "life" or a way out of a certain situation; either way when a bone gets broken or torn your perspective of life changes. I cannot speak on every injury specifically but I can explain the journey of tearing your ACL. I hope it can apply to everyone even if it's not this particular injury. When I tore my ACL, it was the worst pain I ever had to deal with; simply because I didn't know how much I took my legs for granted. It was the aftermath of my surgery which made me realize how much I didn't thank God for the things I thought I had a right to. After surgery, I had to go to my first doctor's appointment. The doctor said, "I want you to lift your leg for me." I tried to lift my leg, but I couldn't; it was at that moment I felt hopeless and cried. I could not move my leg after moving it when I wanted to for my whole life until then. I had to learn how to walk again, gain muscles, run, jump, and just live again. Not only does getting injured break you down physically, it also breaks you down mentally, emotionally, and spiritually.

You have to go to therapy even when you do not want to. You have to push through being depressed and embrace your anger because it can become hard to phantom why God will allow you to go through such agony. However, even when things do not look good, God has good things planned for you. Sometimes you have to sit down and reevaluate your life to understand it is not about you but about helping someone else who is going through a difficult time as well. Martin Luther King Jr. said, "If you cannot run then walk, if you cannot walk then crawl, no matter what the case is just make sure you keep moving." My friend, a setback can never conquer you if you embrace the challenge of making a comeback.

Sincerely,

Comeback

*Letter*
*11*

# *To the Voiceless*

When did you stop giving your voice a sound? Things will not move until you use your voice to shift your situation. When Jesus was on the cross, things did not start to move until He started to speak. Your voice matters. Observe this statement: Jesus actions spoke volume, but it was His words ('It is finished') that transitioned (when the earthquake started) Him to His purpose. In other words, actions can sometimes speak louder than words, but it's the words you speak to yourself that will allow you to reach your purpose. Your energy will start to alter, your soul will get baptized, and the people you attract will no longer drain you, but replenish you.

People will always have something to say, but what makes you shine is you choosing to love yourself first and breathe life back into your existence. Maya Angelou was a mute for a long time. When it was time for her voice to break out it changed her life forever. Speak up and stop living in fear out of concern about what others might say or think about you. The Bible expresses how life and death lies in the power of the tongue; therefore, never lose your voice for it can set you free from the things which keeps you bound. Finally, keep in mind, your voice has the ability to save you from self-destructing, and it is the determination of your strength that will give your voice power.

Sincerely,

Fortitude

*"Poetry is when an emotion has found its thought and the thought has found words."*

*Robert Frost*

*Letter*
*12*

# *To the Broken Poet*

Do you know how powerful you are to the universe? You are the voice for the voiceless and you are the only one who can articulate social issues and problems in a way others cannot. What you have to express matters. Whatever tragedy or circumstances that made your words become shattered; I need you to find the volume of your voice again.

Do you hear the cry of your soul whom wishes to be set free?

Do you see the loss of hope that lies within your dreams?

To express pain in a healthy way is a gift handed to the blessed.

When you suppress your gift, your emotions become unstable & lose conscious on how to rest.

Words are your bond because it represents who you are;

So how dare you let anyone or life take away the creativeness imbedded within your heart.

Scream if you have to. Be silent when necessary.

But no matter what, find your voice again because of the profound strength that it carries.

I love you.

Sincerely,

Words

*Letter*

*13*

# *To the Drunk*

People think you can only become drunk from copious amounts of alcohol without knowing you can become drunk by emotions, which causes one to become unstable. Some of you are drunk from grief, sorrow, anger, hurt, self-pity or negativity and do not even realize it.

Some of you do not understand the side effects of emotional intoxication. You fool yourself to think you are living but in actuality you're just weakly existing. There's a thin line between those who commit suicide and those who are alive but just merely exist. Both are caused by life circumstances; it's just the way they mishandled their pain that makes matters worse for them.

To the ones who live in unwholesome neighborhoods and environments, I hope you will stop becoming drunk from your environment. Your identity does not lie within the conditions of your surroundings. I sincerely ask some of you to stop being drunk from pride. Pain will teach you a lesson but pride will not allow you to learn. Some of you become so filled with pride; it disarms you from reaching your full potential. You see my friend, many think disobedience was the first sin against God, but it was really pride that was the first sin against Him. Do not allow your emotions or pride to lead you down a path for which you have not been purposed. I hope whatever intoxication you've became consumed with, you learn how to meditate on kind, loving, and positive things. Positive energy can reflect who you are. It's time to sober up.

I love you.


Sincerely,

Soberness

*"Our timing is not always the right timing."*

*Unknown*

*Letter 14*

# To the Impatient

Impatience doesn't like to wait on me. It saddens me when you all are so busy being anxious about the future you lose sight to enjoy the present. Listen, the present is all you have; tomorrow does not truly exist since it is not promised. Many of you have lost blessings because you think or believe your agenda is better than God's agenda for your life.

If you do not learn how to be patient, you will lose more than you will gain. You may find yourself rushing into a relationship or a situation simply because of how you feel. Trust Time, not your emotions! It always reveals a more accurate reality. Many hearts would have never required emotional surgery had they waited a while longer. It is incumbent to know masks aren't only worn on Halloween. Remember, just because a blessing is delayed doesn't mean it is denied. Sometimes people can go nowhere really fast.

I love you.


Sincerely,

Time

*Letter*

*15*

# To the Shattered Dreams

Hope becomes broken when your purpose becomes unidentified. Every accomplished dream was birthed through hope. Without hope, you cannot travel to faith. Yes, faith is stronger than hope but without expectation, you can lose sight of living. Every dream started with an imagination, and once you lose your imagination you can forget the meaning of life. Everything you want to do, you can do it; you just have to hope again. If you can hope again you can live again. You have to keep in mind life is not beautiful because of the tangible things; life is beautiful because you never lose hope in the intangible things. You have to learn how to trust God even when you cannot trace Him. Your dreams matter and your hope cannot afford to remain fragile. When God has given you the go, it does not matter what your circumstances are, if you can kneel before Him, you can stand against anyone in power and in strength.

Sincerely,

Faith

*Letter*
*16*

# *To Social Media*

The disconnection between humanity has risen with the spike of usage in social media. It's easy to become something you are not behind a keyboard or phone. Now, before I go any further, I sincerely want to express how social media sites have broadened people's horizons, helped some people careers get started, and allowed many people to connect with others in a healthy way. However, on the other side of the spectrum, nowadays it seem as though likes, views, and comments authenticate who some of you are. Some of you would rather spend time on your phone at dinner or at a family and friends outing, than communicate through verbal dialogue.

The human connection has become increasingly fragile these days. You let comparison steal your joy because you measure your worth and status to what you see on social media. Some of you have even allowed social media to break up healthy relationships; you'd rather find temporary pleasure than talk it out with your partner. Social media is one of the most deceiving souls you will ever encounter.

Many people will puff up their relationships as if they're content before the world but behind the scene they are often the most broken relationships. When you analyze society nowadays, you will see that people would rather pretend and behave as though they are happy, rather than confront who they really are and what they encounter. It's not that being single is a bad thing; it's the false narrative of what being single represents these days. Therefore, the majority of us will submit to being something on social media, even if it does not reflect our circumstances in reality. Social media rarely shows the genuine underpinnings of one's life and romantic relationships. You only see the beginning, the happiness they portray, and the posts they put up when they're upset or have broken up. It is rare to find authentic honest couples to explain that relationships are both loving and hard work.

In conclusion, be mindful on whom you pretend to be because you may forget who you really are. Reflect on this: Who are you without social media? Seriously, who are you? If you did not have over a thousand or million followers, can you really live a life being content with who you are and what you love to do? Remember, young generation, people are more of what they hide than what they show. So, do not get hypnotized with likes and comments; it does not dictate who you are. Do not worship social media my friend. It is better to disconnect yourself from the world than to lose yourself and your humanity within the world.

I love you.


Sincerely,

Connection

*Letter 17*

# *To the Broken Self-Image*

Sometimes we do not know how much weight we are carrying until we let it go. Broken images can birth themselves from many places. Whether you are overweight, undersize, gorgeous or think otherwise; if you do not see your worth whenever you look in the mirror then you are broken. Mirrors do not lie, especially the ones that reflect who we are on the inside. The deceptions come from your eyes and what you think of yourself. Your mind and eyes have to be cleansed and renewed every day. Your mentality is the source of changing your image and your eyes are the production of keeping your image.

The thief of joy is unhealthy comparison. When you compare yourself to someone who seems to represent the "world standard" of beauty then you devalue your self-worth to false ideals. Sometimes the most beautiful people in the world have the ugliest heart. You cannot help the features you were born with. Having a kind and loving soul can make someone including yourself look 10 times more beautiful than those who seem to have inherited a "perfect body." You are not ugly; it's the brokenness you have allowed to identify you that has affected how you see yourself. If you do not think you are worthy of love then no one else is going to value you.

Finally, to my black girls, especially the young ones, no matter if you are dark-skin, light-skin, or caramel you are beautiful and do not let the "plantation mentality" affect how you view yourself. Recite an encouraging line to yourself every day until you believe the beauty of those words reflect who are. Remember no one can make you feel inferior without your consent. So, get up, embrace who you are, and change the things you can because God did not make a mistake when He painted you.

I love you.

Sincerely,

Worthiness

*"To be in your children's memories tomorrow, you have to be in their lives today."*

*Anonymous*

*Letter 18*

# To the Absent Father and Mother

Man was the first human God created and therefore, I believe men are my descendants. Fathers have such a powerful role in the human race and in the foundation of families. Generally speaking, fathers are their daughters' first lovers and their son's first real model. When a father is absent from their child's life, they create a void and an imbalance that is hard to shift back in place.

A woman cannot modify what it means to be a man but they can edify the importance on becoming a great man. There are so many girls out here in the world looking for love in all the wrong places because they end up dating their father. They are looking for a man when the man they "found" is still a boy, and the girl eventually lose the importance of who she is simply because many of them did not have their father to tell them their worth. On the other hand, there are many young men who are angry and turn to the streets to find their identity as a man rather than becoming the opposite of their pain to push them to be a better man than their father. Overall, people especially children reflect the absence of a parent than the possibility of hope of a better future for themselves.

When it comes to a mother being absent from a child's life, it damages the essence of their soul. Our soul is our emotions and when our emotions are not nurtured, our pain is not validated. A mother brings love to a hopeless place and calmness in uneasy storms. I understand all mothers are not superheroes or great, but a majority of them are. Mothers bring validation to their sons and add value to their daughters being. God gave mothers the ability to help shift the imbalance of when the father is absence because the proof is when you see how so many young boys become great fathers; not because their father was in their life but because their mothers became the courage they needed to live on anyhow. Therefore, I recommend you all to get it together as parents since many children become the reflection of their first home.

I love you.

Sincerely,

Reflection

*"It is easier to build strong children than to repair broken men."*

Frederick Douglas

*Letter 19*

# To the Motherless and Fatherless Child

Sometimes we look at things the wrong way. It's easier to get angry at pain you don't take time out to understand. It's hard for anyone to give something they never had; they can only learn in due time. Your pain, your tears, and thoughts need to be heard from your absent parent. Let them know you're angry because behind anger is hurt.

Sometimes we don't know why things happen the way that they do but what if your parent was around, would you be the same person you are today? What I mean by this statement is sometimes it may be a blessing in disguise; maybe their absence promoted your purpose so you would not pick up negative behaviors that God did not want you to learn. This is not justifying or implying you have no right to feel the pain you feel; but only suggesting trying to look at things in a different way.

No wound can heal if you keep it covered up, especially since it hinders your growth and your ability to forgive. For those of you who turn to the streets or trying to fill a void because daddy or mommy was not around, I can only ask you to find your identity in your pain for it's there where your destiny lies. You might have to go back and heal the little boy or girl inside of you, so childish behavior will not transpire when you become older. You're not bitter, you're just hurt. You're not a thug, you just don't know any better. However, I believe in you! I know you have the courage to walk away from the negative emotions that can lead you down a dangerous path.

Finally, I am fully aware not everyone's mother or father abandoned them, but just transitioned to another life too early. I recommend you read the others letters, since only time and prayer can help you cope with your loss. I want you to know your angel is still with you on the inside. They want you to LEARN how to live on because throwing in the towel is not an option. Their legacy lives on through you and the children you will bear if you decide to have any. Do not give up but embrace the weeping you have to endure, in order to get the joy you need to smile and live again.

I love you.

Sincerely,

Validation

*Letter*
*20*

# *To the One Who Has Been Church Hurt*

I heard they hurt you and violated you in My name. I want to be the first to tell you I am sorry for your experience and what you had to endure. I realize in your eyes, many "Christians" seem to rehearse being a hypocrite rather than being committed to being transparent in their spiritual walk. You cannot heal from what you refuse to address; the church can never move forward diligently or publically, until they go back and confront the wounds they created privately.

I am so sorry for how some pastors, ministers, team leaders, and just members in general treated you in your time of need and despair. It is wrong for someone to take advantage of you physically, mentally, emotionally, and spiritually when you are vulnerable and seeking guidance or comfort. I want to make Myself very clear My child, I am not for the hurt people injected into you, however, I am for the redemption and peace that they stole away from you. Through loving kindness did I draw thee, and only through transparency will I keep thee. Walking an authentic Christ-like journey is not easy but it is definitely worth it. Some days you will get mad at Me, and you will not always be in the mood to pray or talk to Me, but I will never leave you nor forsake you even when life circumstances make you feel as though I have.

Overall My child, the people in the church are not perfect; no one is. Some are wolves in sheep clothing and others are good hearts with human flaws, but both need a Savior (Me). I love you, I truly do, and I can only hope you learn to love me again not through the eyes of flawed people, but through the eyes of honest healing. I am here for you and always will be here for you, even if you never return to the place that made you lose faith in Me in the first place.

I love you.

Sincerely,
Jesus the Carpenter

*"No matter how big your church is, your ego is not more important than God's mission."*

*SWAG*

*Letter*
*21*

# To the Broken Pastor

Sometimes the best way to feel connected to God is to remember the reason why you need God. As a pastor, a preacher, or minister, I hope you understand your purpose in life is to plant seeds and allow them to grow. There are different kinds of people in the pulpit: the great ones, the crooked ones, the entitled ones, and the overwhelming ones. One of my favorite things I like to say is you have to embrace the humanity component of a person so they will be open to the divinity side of things. Until you address or acknowledge people's pain, many will not be open to what God can offer.

Many of you carry the weight of so many people's sins and burdens, to the point you have no room to regenerate the energy you need to be helpful. It is the anointing on your life which makes you seem better than what you actually are. Therefore, it is imperative you seek God and replenish your soul. The gift you have is not man-made but God-given. Sometimes my friend, you have to separate yourself from people to make sure your soul is intact. Even Jesus took time out for Himself; even though He was 100% divine, He was 100% human as well. In other words, embrace the talent but enhance the gift of which you have to offer to this world.

Embrace your tiredness, your frustration, your anger, your disappointments, your shortcomings, your weariness, and your brokenness. You are not God; you are just His mere creation and a child who will forever need the Creator to renew them. Know that prayer still works better than you. You cannot be everything to everybody. Remember, people will kill you, if you let them. If no one has told you lately you are treasured, you are doing a fantastic job leading and serving others. Even if you have made a mistake and feel like David, you are still loved in His sight, near to His thoughts, and tied to His heart. Finally, recognize the more God wants to use you; the more the enemy wants to destroy you. The enemy disguises himself in many forms; therefore, I encourage you to take solace my friend in knowing whose you are and who you are. If you have assisted someone along the way, or brought someone closer to Jesus, then, Heaven is proud of you and is rejoicing.

Sincerely,

Relief

*Letter*
*22*

# *To the One Holding a Grudge*

One reason why people like to hold a grudge against someone else is because of the leverage they may have over them. As humans, we all have a knack for holding things over someone else's head, when we really have no right to do so. Holding a grudge will suffocate you; it can kill your opportunity to release the angst that will eventually grant you peace. In other words, it is easier to hold on to the hurt we think motivates us rather than inviting the peace that can elevate us.

To forgive means you give up the right to seek revenge. Embrace your hurt and the situation that made you upset, but let it go. Letting something go does not make you weak but symbolizes strength. Forgiveness renews your soul and refreshes your heart. So many of you are blocking your blessings because of the malice you hold within your spirit. You are not perfect so you cannot expect someone else to be either. What if God treated us the way we treat each other? I am not implying forgiveness means you always give people second chances to be in your life, but it does mean you give yourself permission to breathe again. How people treat you is their karma and how you react is yours.

I love you.

Sincerely,

Forgiveness

*"Love has no limits, but it does have boundaries."*

*Unknown*

*Letter 23*

# *To the Broken Love (relationships)*

Love is a beautiful thing wouldn't you say? As humans you all tend to put your own definition to the meaning of love. The reason why many romantic couples fail in this day and age is because of their lack of understanding on what love really is. In humanity, you all try to limit love to your perspective when in reality it's beyond you. Love does not feel as though it is entitled to anything. Love does not try to prove points as to who is right and who is wrong but it seeks the line of understanding on what you can do for the other person. Relationships also fail because there's so much entertainment around you to distract you when things do not necessarily go your way. You cannot sleep with everyone. Your work cannot bring you comfort when you are not having the best day and the grass is not always greener on the other side. If you are not careful, you will find yourself leaving someone who is worth keeping, over someone who does not value your imperfections but only reaps the benefits of you becoming a butterfly.

On the other hand, I've noticed humans do not appreciate kindness. It's as if you all have become consumed with mistreatment; therefore, when genuine love is given to you it makes you uncomfortable. You will fight for someone simply because you have history with them not because of how they value your worth as a human being. Some of you allow your "friends" to influence your thinking. When you start to invite others into your relationship, you can put your relationship in jeopardy. This is not implying that advice shouldn't be sought at times when dealing with some situations, but do not express everything to everybody especially without informing your significant other about it first. Seek advice from someone who wants to see you succeed, not someone who envies you in disguise.

Sometimes people can dismiss love when they've been shown the wrong definition of what love really is. Understand many people do not want love; they just want someone to fill their void, since love is not really valued but for some just entertainment. Love is pure and authentic, not self-seeking. When you truly love somebody you work it out especially when their good outweighs their bad. Once you truly comprehend how love operates the easier the process becomes. You have to understand your worth, in order to love someone healthy in a romantic relationship. When you do not know your worth, you end up settling for the love you think you deserve. So, I simply recommend you grasp the value of love so you won't lose the meaning of it.

I love you.


Sincerely,

Understanding

*Letter*
*24*

# *To the Broken Heart*

Everything you lose is not a loss. This letter may not be long but it will be necessary for you. Some things are not meant to destroy you but only to prepare you for the next season in your life. Relationships, especially romantic ones, can take a toll on us the most. We tend to open our hearts to the ones who were never designed to cherish it. Some of us particularly the loyal ones, will stay in a place where our hearts are no longer appreciated; since mistreatment is all we understand sometimes. It's okay to fight for someone who loves you, but it is never okay to fight for someone to love you. If you are not careful, you will find yourself at a very low point in your life, and will try to end yourself because your significant partner at the time didn't care enough to change their behavior for you.

It's sad to say this but it is true: some people just do not care what they do to others as long as the other person's actions are beneficial to them. People will manipulate you and use you if you let them. You set the tone for how you want others to treat you. Do not allow people to use their brokenness as an excuse to mistreat or manipulate you. Sometimes we cannot control what breaks us in life but we can choose to remain broken by those tragedies. Whenever a person can see how much their actions are affecting you and doesn't change, trust me they do not care about you. Some people are selfish, some people are cold, and many people are broken but you have to love yourself enough to want better. At the end of the day my friend, NO MAN OR WOMAN IS WORTH YOUR LIFE. Remember, it is a choice to stay broken and it is a decision to want to live. God has something better waiting for you, you just have to be willing to love yourself enough to walk away from the thing/person who is causing you the most pain. I love you and even baby steps count as progress.

Sincerely,

Let it go.

*"Forgiveness will free you from the pain that was designed to kill you."*

*SWAG*

# To the Violated

There are two types of rape victims: the ones who get raped mentally and those who get taken advantage of physically. This is for both men and women who have been violated or sexually abused in any way; it is time to get your life back. Whomever took advantage of you has no right to your joy and how you think of yourself. Statistically it is said, people who become rapists or violators have been a victim of sexual abuse as well. However, it does not give them a right or a pass to have sexually abused and violated your humanity. No means "no" and what happened to you is not your fault.

When you are sexually abused it leaves a stain on your soul. When your perpetrator made you feel defenseless, your power became lost. You have to take your aptitude back; your soul does not belong to your victimization. The first step of getting your power back is grasping why it is missing in the first place. When someone robs you of who you are, they gain the ability to replace you with what you're not. The nightmares are real and the numbness you feel is justified, but if you do not get up and choose to live my love, then your perpetrator will always lay next to you.

Remember love, some tragedies aren't meant for your destruction, but for your development.

Sincerely,

Power

*"Being a parent is not easy; however, your response is imperative to your child's healing in their time of need and despair. Do not neglect them, when they need your love the most."*

*SWAG*

*Letter*
*26*

# *To the Broken Parent*

Some things are not in your control. I want to acknowledge being a parent is not easy and there are so many things you have to endure and learn. There is no manual on how to be a great parent. However, I want to talk to the parent who is dealing with a child who is gay and you do not know how to handle it; whether you are spiritual or not you all have hopes and dreams for your children to be married to the opposite gender and to be happy. The image of them being with the same gender never truly crosses your mind. However, beating them up mom and dad, is not going to save them, it's going to push them away and make them deaf to your hurt. You should not be ashamed or have any type of resentment towards your child because of whaever your personal beliefs may be. If your theology makes you deny and treat your child with hate then you need a new theology.

At the end of the day that is your child. I am not saying you have to approve or change your beliefs but you do have to change your heart. Your child maybe thinking about suicide; not only are they dealing with the shame from the outside world, or getting bullied at school, but they're also getting beat up by the same people who are supposed to love them despite of their flaws like God does with you. Can you imagine God denying you and only loving you conditionally? I know it's not the norm and I know it can be hurtful but if you can love them despite of it all, that's when you will really experience the love of Christ in your heart. Not only will your ears open up to the hate your child receives but it will humble your heart to the love they so desperately need. I pray you hear my heart on this because it may just save your child's life and a family bond.

I love you.


Sincerely

Unconditional Love

*"God does not rank sin; only man."*

*SWAG*

*Letter*
*27*

# To the Unaccepted One

Hey you. The one struggling with your sexuality or maybe even embracing your sexuality; how are you? If you're doing well, I want you to be doing better, and if you are not doing so well I pray you will be after reading this letter. I don't know if you are religious or not but at this point of time it does not matter because you both are human.

For the one who does have some type of faith in a higher power, I want you to know that God does not like sin but He loves you. I know you are struggling and maybe even being condemned to hell for that matter, but God loves you, He just doesn't like our sins. It was a reason why He sacrificed His Son Jesus; He was the only One who could pay a debt we could never repay. You see, God will give up His Son before He gives up on you.

This is not a letter to justify anything but this is a letter to lift you up and bring back your humanity. Just because some may look at you like a disease, God views you as a horizon and sunset. You see a horizon/sunset is very beautiful but what brings the color to display is dirt and pollution. What I am trying to say is that the trials and struggles in life make us who we are, but the sunset and the horizon you watch is a reflection of our reality. It's the ugly things in life that make us cry and make us feel shameful but its overcoming those things that shines us up and make us beautiful.

Even for the one who is not religious, the lack of unconditional love you may feel, and acceptance you may be longing for can make you feel worthless but I am here to tell you, you are not. Speak your hurt until it is heard. You matter, even when people or people in the church try to use Scriptures or cruel words to demonstrate that you don't.

As I close this letter, I truly do pray for peace in your life and that you do not let the things people say or do kill you. You have meaning, you have purpose, and you are loved. However, with that being said I have to keep it authentic with you by saying, it is okay for your loves ones, or even kind strangers to disagree or not approve of your preference or lifestyle but it is not okay for them to show you a lack of unconditional love. Therefore, the brokenness you may feel on the inside does not keep you away from God, it attracts Him. I love you but God loves you because that's just who He is.

Sincerely,

Love

*Letter*
*28*

# *Closing Letter*

I want to first thank you for reading every letter even if you may have disagreed or gained a broader perspective on a subject. Life is life and sometimes it's fair and other times it's not, but regardless of the circumstances you will notice that *living is still an option.* I rather die trying to live than exist and never lived at all. All of us are broken in some type of way; therefore, it would be wise to keep in mind that some people are not bad, they're just broken. Everyone does not cope with pain the same way; yet healing is still available to us all. Healing may not always be comfortable but growth will forever be necessary. I love you and as I always say. "We are in this together."

# *About the Author*

The author was born and raised in Miami, FL. She is a Child of God and a lover of people. She has a Bachelor's Degree in Counseling & Human Services with plans to obtain a Master's degree in counseling. She is a product of love and imperfection. She is also a daughter, a sister, a friend, a niece, a basketball coach, and more. She does not condone hate or any form of corruption. She has a genuine soul that cares for the community and the well-being of people. She is **Dareyelle Avant.**

# *Upcoming Books:*

- *Beyond the Hoodie*
- *Dear Broken Black Child*
- *Inside the game of life*
- *Your Perspective Can Kill You*

www.ingramcontent.com/pod-product-compliance
Lightning Source LLC
La Vergne TN
LVHW021520080426
835509LV00018B/2578